Trains Coloring Book Mosaic Color By Number Locomotives on the Railroads and Railways Steam Engines and Electric Train Art For Stress Relief and Relaxation

By Color Questopia

Copyright © 2020

All rights reserved. No part of this publication may be reproduced, distributed, or transmitted in any form or by any means, including photocopying, recording, or other electronic or mechanical methods, without the prior written permission of the publisher

Color By Number Tips

1. **Relax and have fun**
   Let your cares slip away as you color the images. Take your time. Coloring is a meditative activity and there's no wrong way to do it. Feel free to color as you listen to music, watch TV, lounge in bed- do whatever relaxes you most! You can also color while you're out and about- on the train or at a cafe- take the book with you anywhere you go. Coloring is therapeutic and is great for stress relief and relaxation!

2. **Colors corresponding to each number are shown on the back cover of the book**
   Each number corresponds to a color shown on the back of the book. You can match the color as closely as you like- but feel free to change the color or the shade if you don't have the exact color match- that's totally fine. Although this is a color by number book, it's completely okay to get creative and color the images with whichever colors you like and have. The numbers are there to be a guide and to allow you to color without having to focus your energy on choosing colors.

3. **Choose your coloring tools**
   Everyone has their favorite coloring markers, crayons, pencils, pens- even paints! Feel free to color with any tool that you like! If you choose markers or paints, we recommend putting a blank sheet of paper or cardboard behind each image, so that your colors don't run onto the next image.

1. Brown
2. Dark Brown
3. Beige
4. Yellow
5. Red
6. Blue
7. Medium Orange
8. Medium Gray
9. Dark Blue
10. Dark Gray
11. Light Brown
12. Medium Blue
13. Soft Violet
14. Green
15. Medium Green
16. Light Green
17. Light Gray
18. White
19. Light Blue
20. Sky Blue

1. Brown
2. Dark Gray
3. Navy Blue
4. Medium Gray
5. Light Gray
6. Dark Red
7. Medium Orange
8. Medium Blue
9. Gray
10. Army Green
11. Light Violet
12. Green
13. Medium Green
14. Light Green
15. Neon Green
16. Light Blue
17. White
18. Sky Blue

1. Dark Brown
2. Orange
3. Navy Blue
4. Dark Gray
5. Red
6. Medium Gray
7. Light Gray
8. Gray
9. Green
10. Blue
11. Light Violet
12. Medium Orange
13. Dark Blue
14. Dark Yellow
15. Medium Red
16. Violet
17. White
18. Sky Blue
19. Light Blue

1. Violet
2. Yellow
3. Beige
4. Dark Brown
5. Brown
6. Light Green
7. Green
8. Dark Green
9. Gray
10. Medium Gray
11. Medium Green
12. Medium Orange
13. Red
14. Medium Red
15. Dark Yellow
16. Orange
17. Blue
18. Light Blue
19. White
20. Sky Blue

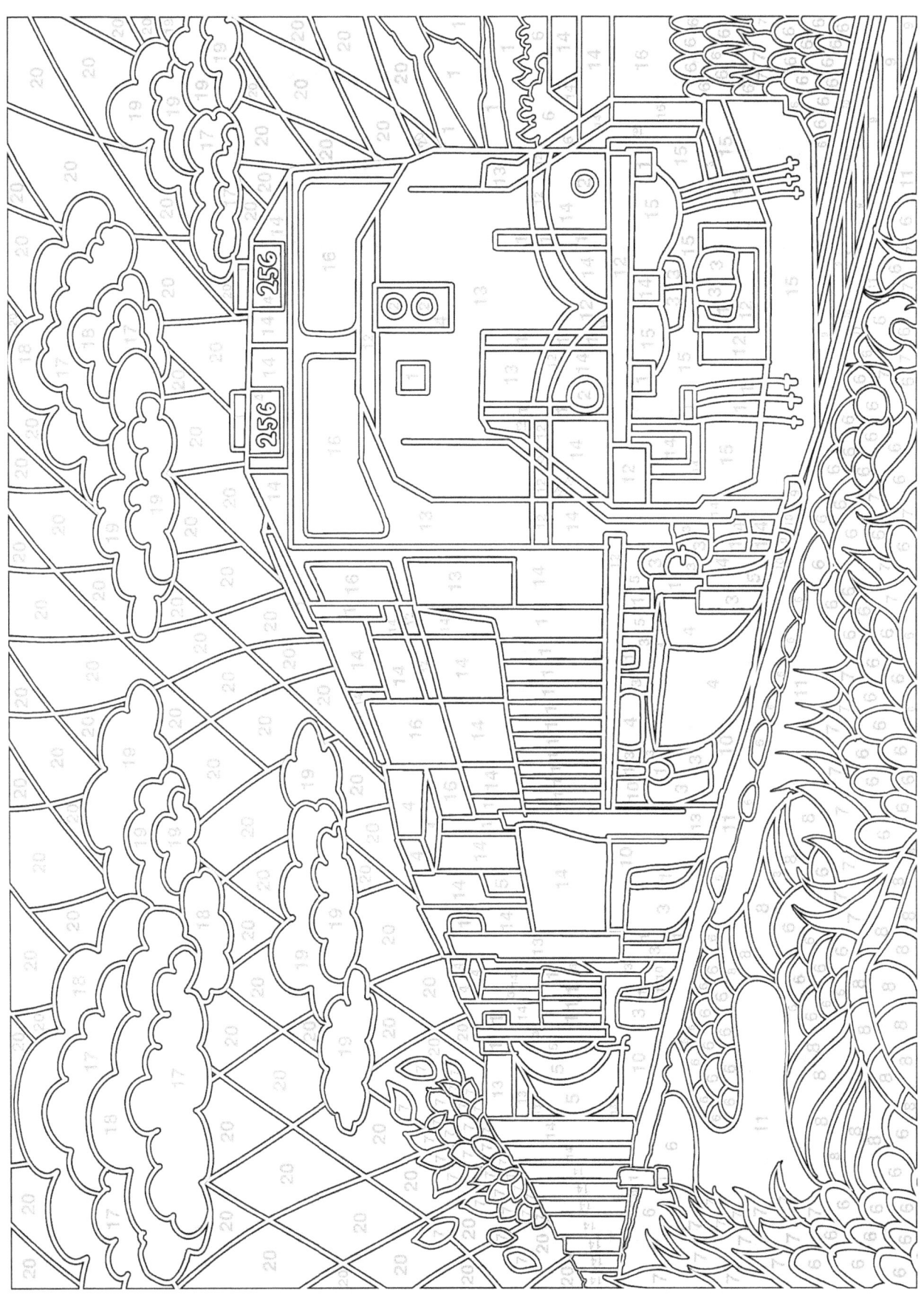

1. Light Green
2. Green
3. Medium Green
4. Medium Gray
5. Dark Gray
6. Violet
7. Gray
8. Medium Orange
9. Light Gray
10. Medium Red
11. Red
12. Medium Blue
13. Brown
14. Blue
15. Medium Brown
16. Yellow
17. Light Blue
18. Sky Blue

1. Dark Yellow
2. Medium Gray
3. Gray
4. Dark Gray
5. Green
6. Light Green
7. Dark Green
8. Army Green
9. Blue
10. Yellow
11. Light Violet
12. Violet
13. Navy Blue
14. Brown
15. Soft Violet
16. Red
17. Light Gray
18. Sky Blue

1. Dark Green
2. Green
3. Neon Green
4. Army Green
5. Medium Green
6. Light Green
7. Medium Orange
8. Light Brown
9. Dark Blue
10. Red
11. Gray
12. Medium Blue
13. Yellow
14. Dark Gray
15. Blue
16. Light Gray
17. Medium Gray
18. Sky Blue
19. Light Blue

1. Medium Green
2. Light Green
3. Army Green
4. Dark Green
5. Medium Gray
6. Gray
7. Light Gray
8. Dark Gray
9. Medium Orange
10. Yellow
11. Dark Blue
12. Light Blue
13. Medium Blue
14. Violet
15. Red
16. Blue
17. Sky Blue

1. Medium Gray
2. Dark Red
3. Purple
4. Gray
5. Light Gray
6. Dark Blue
7. Medium Orange
8. Red
9. Dark Brown
10. Dark Gray
11. Violet
12. Medium Blue
13. Blue
14. Medium Purple
15. Green
16. Light Green
17. Neon Green
18. White
19. Sky Blue

1. Violet
2. Blue
3. Beige
4. Yellow
5. Medium Gray
6. Medium Blue
7. Orange
8. Light Orange
9. Pink
10. Light Pink
11. Light Violet
12. Soft Violet
13. Dark Yellow
14. Gray
15. Dark Gray
16. Light Gray
17. Light Blue
18. Light Brown
19. Brown

1. Brown
2. Light Brown
3. Gray
4. Dark Gray
5. Light Blue
6. Orange
7. Purple
8. Dark Yellow
9. Medium Red
10. Blue
11. Soft Violet
12. Medium Blue
13. Beige
14. Medium Brown
15. Violet
16. Medium Orange
17. Medium Purple
18. Navy Blue

1. Brown
2. Medium Gray
3. Light Gray
4. Dark Gray
5. Dark Red
6. Gray
7. Medium Orange
8. Soft Violet
9. Dark Blue
10. Yellow
11. Red
12. Violet
13. Blue
14. Light Violet
15. Purple
16. Medium Brown
17. Medium Red
18. White
19. Light Green
20. Sky Blue

1. Black
2. Dark Gray
3. Navy Blue
4. Light Brown
5. Brown
6. Green
7. Medium Green
8. Light Green
9. Army Green
10. Light Gray
11. Gray
12. Dark Yellow
13. Violet
14. Blue
15. Red
16. Medium Orange
17. Light Blue
18. Baby Blue
19. Sky Blue

1. Dark Red
2. Orange
3. Dark Gray
4. Gray
5. Medium Gray
6. Light Gray
7. Red
8. Light Green
9. Dark Blue
10. Brown
11. Medium Blue
12. Blue
13. Medium Orange
14. Yellow
15. Green
16. Light Brown
17. Medium Red
18. Dark Yellow
19. White
20. Sky Blue

1. Gray
2. Dark Gray
3. Light Gray
4. Medium Gray
5. Medium Orange
6. Light Brown
7. Dark Orange
8. White
9. Medium Brown
10. Yellow
11. Medium Blue
12. Red
13. Violet
14. Orange
15. Blue
16. Medium Red
17. Army Green
18. Green
19. Sky Blue

1. Gray
2. Dark Gray
3. Light Gray
4. Medium Gray
5. Orange
6. Medium Brown
7. Brown
8. Green
9. Dark Blue
10. Yellow
11. Medium Red
12. Red
13. Medium Orange
14. Medium Blue
15. Light Brown
16. Blue
17. Medium Green
18. Light Green
19. Army Green
20. Sky Blue

1. Gray
2. Medium Gray
3. Dark Gray
4. Gray
5. Dark Brown
6. Dark Orange
7. Medium Orange
8. Red
9. Dark Blue
10. Blue
11. Light Violet
12. Violet
13. Soft Violet
14. Green
15. Dark Pink
16. Orange
17. Army Green
18. Green
19. Light Green
20. Sky Blue

1. Light Brown
2. Brown
3. Dark Brown
4. Dark Orange
5. Red
6. Gray
7. Dark Gray
8. Light Gray
9. Medium Gray
10. Yellow
11. Orange
12. Medium Blue
13. Dark Blue
14. Violet
15. Medium Brown
16. Army Green
17. Light Green
18. White
19. Sky Blue

1. Dark Red
2. Dark Blue
3. Gray
4. Medium Gray
5. Light Gray
6. Dark Gray
7. Blue
8. Medium Blue
9. Medium Purple
10. Yellow
11. Red
12. Orange
13. Light Brown
14. Medium Brown
15. Dark Brown
16. Brown
17. Soft Violet
18. Beige
19. Light Green
20. Sky Blue

1. Brown
2. Medium Gray
3. Dark Gray
4. Blue
5. Light Gray
6. Gray
7. Dark Orange
8. Medium Brown
9. Light Violet
10. Yellow
11. Light Red
12. Medium Orange
13. Light Brown
14. Red
15. Green
16. Light Green
17. White
18. Sky Blue

ENJOY BONUS IMAGES FROM SOME OF OUR OTHER FUN COLOR BY NUMBER BOOKS!

FIND ALL OF OUR BOOKS ON AMAZON

Beautiful Cities and Landmarks
Color by Number
Mosaic World Geography
Coloring Book For Adults

1. Medium Gray
2. Dark Gray
3. Gray
4. Purple
5. Light Gray
6. Green
7. Neon Green
8. Army Green
9. Brown
10. Light Orange
11. Beige
12. Light Blue
13. Baby Blue
14. Navy Blue
15. Light Pink
16. Yellow
17. Hot Pink
18. Medium Blue

Country Farm Scenes
Nature, Animal, and Easy Designs
Adult Coloring Book
Color By Number For Adults

1. Red
2. Dark Red
3. Pink
4. Dark Brown
5. Red
6. Yellow
7. Dark Green
8. Medium Green
9. Army Green
10. Green
11. Light Green
12. Light Brown
13. Brown
14. Gray
15. Light Gray
16. Blue
17. Light Blue

Dragon Fantasy
Mosaic Color By Number
Mythical Magic and Lore for Stress Relief

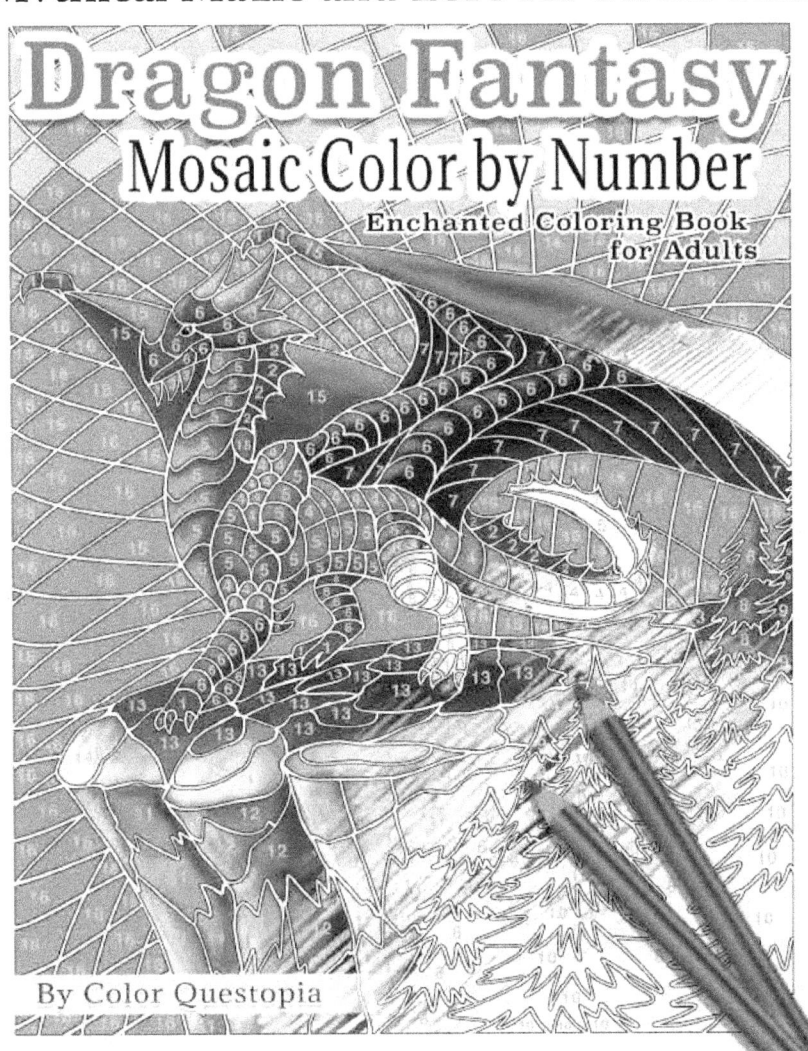

1. Dark Brown
2. Light Pink
3. Red
4. Orange
5. Dark Orange
6. Dark Yellow
7. Light Orange
8. Yellow
9. Brown
10. Army Green
11. Light Brown
12. Blue
13. Light Green
14. Violet
15. Sky Blue
16. Baby Blue
17. Light Blue

Creative Movie Posters
Color By Number
Mosaic Movie Images and Scenes

1. Black
2. Brown
3. Dark Yellow
4. White
5. Dark Brown
6. Gray
7. Yellow
8. Dark Gray
9. Orange
10. Light Orange
11. Peach
12. Blue
13. Green
14. Red
15. Light Violet
16. Violet
17. Dark Green
18. Sky Blue

Horses Jumbo Adult Coloring Book
Horses and Ponies Grazing and Racing
Color by Number

1. Yellow
2. Light Brown
3. Dark brown
4. Light Red
5. Brown
6. Dark Orange
7. Orange
8. Dark Red
9. Light Yellow
10. Yellow
11. White
12. Black
13. Light green
14. green
15. Army Green
16. Light blue
17. Navy Blue
18. Sky Blue
19. Dark blue

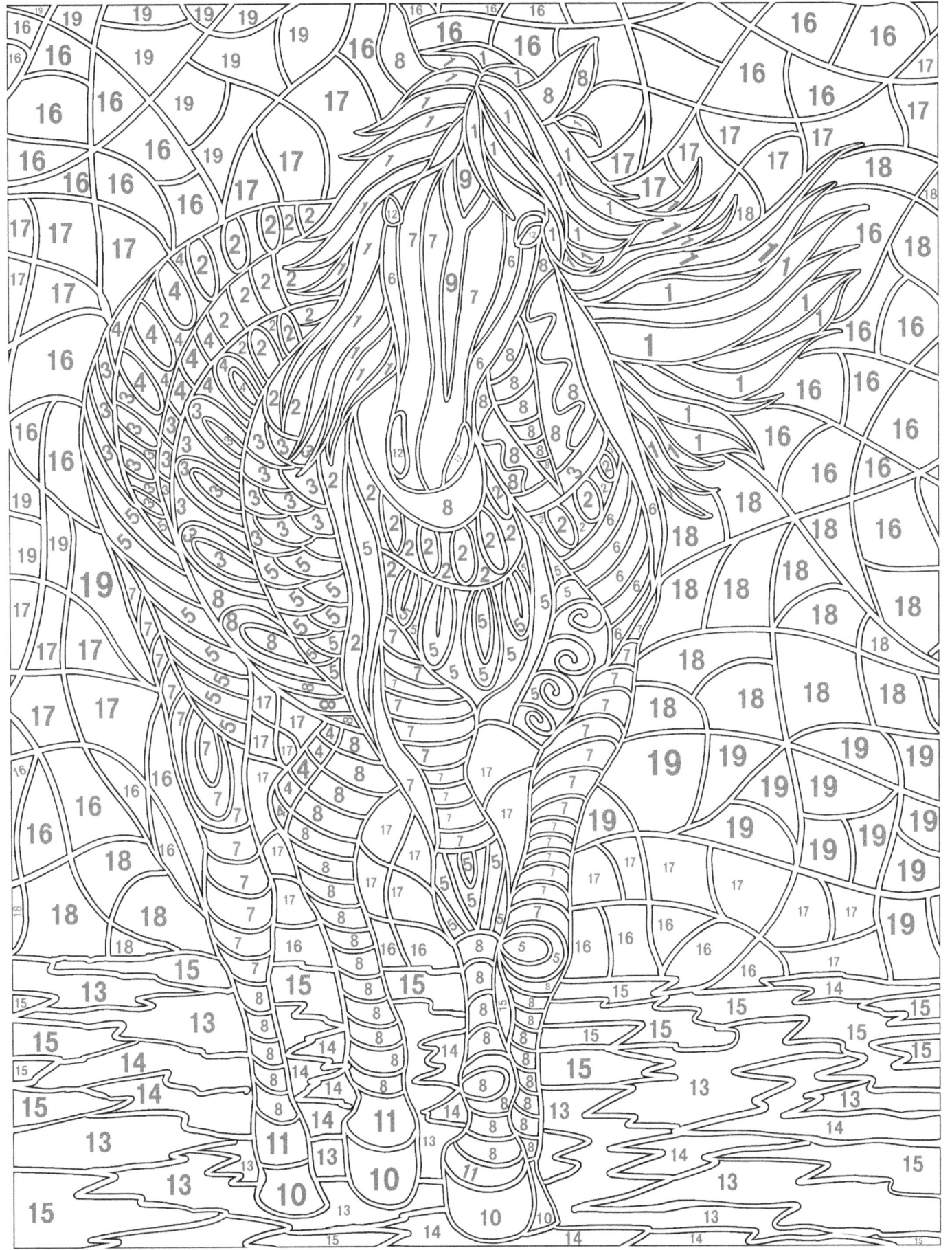

www.ingramcontent.com/pod-product-compliance
Lightning Source LLC
Chambersburg PA
CBHW080525220526
45465CB00006B/2601